D1217273

THE WORLD
OF NASCAR

DALE EARNHARDT:
The Likable Intimidator

BY PHIL BARBER

T TRADITION BOOKS™
EXCELSIOR, MINNESOTA

Published by **Tradition Books**™ and distributed to the
school and library market by **The Child's World**®
P.O. Box 326
Chanhassen, MN 55317-0326
800/599-READ
http://www.childsworld.com

Photo Credits
Cover and title page: Sports Gallery/Tom Riles (left) and Sports
  Gallery/Brian Cleary (right)
Allsport: 22; 23, 25 (Robert Laberge); 26, 29 (Jonathan Ferrey);
AP/Wide World: 7, 9, 12, 13, 14, 18, 24
Sports Gallery: 1, 5, 11 (Tom Riles); 1, 8, 19 (Brian Cleary);
  4 (Joe Robbins); 15, 17 (Brian Spurlock)
Sports Immortals, Inc.: 20

Book production by Shoreline Publishing Group, LLC
Art direction and design by The Design Lab

Library of Congress Cataloging-in-Publication Data

Barber, Phil.
  Dale Earnhardt : the likable intimidator / by Phil Barber.
     p. cm. — (The world of NASCAR series)
Includes bibliographical references (p.   ) and index.
  ISBN 1-59187-001-1 (lib. bdg. : alk. paper)
  1. Earnhardt, Dale, 1951– —Juvenile literature. 2. Automobile racing drivers—United
States—Biography—Juvenile literature. [1. Earnhardt, Dale, 1951– 2. Automobile racing
drivers.] I. Title. II. Series.
  GV1032.E18 B37 2002
  796.72—dc21   2002004640

Printed in the United States of America.

D A L E   E A R N H A R D T

Table of Contents

4   **Introduction:** Something Is Missing

6   **Chapter One:** Born to Race

10   **Chapter Two:** A Storybook Career

16   **Chapter Three:** Just a Good Old Boy

21   **Chapter Four:** A Dark Day for Racing

29   Dale Earnhardt's Life

30   Glossary

31   For More Information about Dale Earnhardt

32   Index

INTRODUCTION

Something Is Missing

Something was missing during the 2001 NASCAR season. The circuit had plenty of great races, skillful drivers, and super-fast cars. But for the first time in 23 years, it didn't have Dale Earnhardt.

Some say Dale was the greatest racer of all time. From 1979 through 2000, he was never far from the top of the NASCAR standings. When he crashed and died in the Daytona 500 on February 18, 2001, it was almost too terrible to be true.

As fellow driver Mike Wallace said after the event, "He was what we are all trying to be on the racetrack, and he was

NASCAR fans have said goodbye to Dale Earnhardt, but they'll never forget him.

what we would like to be off the track, too."

Behind the wheel, Dale Earnhardt was just about the toughest racer you've ever seen. He never backed down. He wasn't afraid to give opponents a "love tap" or two to send a message. Away from the speedway, though, Dale was friendly and popular. He usually had a smile shining from beneath his bushy mustache. He always found time for kids and young drivers.

Race fans will never forget the Man in Black, and they sure will miss his driving.

Earnhardt loved being in the thick of the action, dueling side-by-side with other racers.

C H A P T E R   O N E

Born to Race

As a boy, Dale Earnhardt spent a lot of time with his dad. They usually weren't fishing or playing catch or watching TV, though. They were working on **stock cars.**

Ralph Earnhardt was one of the best drivers of his day. He raced on dirt tracks most weekends, usually not far from the family's home in Kannapolis, North Carolina. Ralph won more than 500 races in 23 years. He was inducted into the National Motorsports Press Association Hall of Fame in 1989.

"I think I watched every foot of every lap he ever ran after I started going to races with him and mom," Dale said at an awards banquet in 1990. "And I was almost always at his elbow there in the garage in the back of our yard, trying to see what he did that made his cars so strong."

Ralph had grown up in a house on Sedan Street. He

turned an old barn into a garage, and that's where he would

tinker with his race cars. Dale's mother, Martha, still lives in

the house, but Ralph died in 1973. He had a heart attack while

working on a car in that very same garage.

Dale was still a teenager when he began racing **Hobby-**

class cars near Kannapolis. He worked full-time during the

week, attended to his cars at night, and raced on weekends.

Dale entered his first **Winston Cup** race in 1975 when

he was only 24 years old. The race was the World 600 at

Charlotte Motor Speedway, and he finished twenty-second.

Dale crossed the finish line one spot ahead of Richard

Ralph Earnhardt raced anything with four wheels.
Here he's bumping around in a convertible race.

Childress. Childress would become Dale's partner in racing for many years.

Dale entered a few Winston Cup races in 1976, but he didn't really get serious until 1979. He earned his first Winston Cup victory that year, in the Southeastern 500 at Bristol, Tennessee. It was only his sixteenth professional start. Dale went on to score 11 top-five finishes in 1979 and was named NASCAR's Rookie of the Year.

After winning at Bristol, Dale said, "I know that somewhere there's a fellow that's got a great big smile and is mighty, mighty proud and even more happy than I am, if that's possible."

Everybody knew he was talking about his dad.

Car owner Richard Childress and Dale made a powerful racing team.

PRETTY (AND) INTIMIDATING

They called Dale Earnhardt "The **Intimidator.**" But believe it or not, this tough guy's first race car was pink. He and his father, Ralph, and some family friends had fixed up a 1956 Ford. They wanted to paint it purple, but they didn't get the mixture quite right, and the car came out pink. They didn't have enough money to repaint it, so Dale just laughed and got behind the wheel.

Dale may have started in a pink car, but his color scheme was light blue for this 1979 victory.

CHAPTER TWO

A Storybook Career

N ot everyone agrees on just who is the greatest stock-car racer of all time. Some experts and fans insist it's Richard Petty, who won a record 200 races in his NASCAR career. Others swear it's the current favorite, Jeff Gordon, who won four Winston Cup titles before the age of 31. But fans who grew up watching NASCAR in the 1980s will tell you the answer is Dale Earnhardt.

In 1980, a year after he was rookie of the year, Dale won five races and captured his first Winston Cup championship; he's still the only driver to win those awards in back-to-back years.

Dale had a disappointing 1981 season, winning no races and earning no **poles** that year. Looking back, though, it was a big year for him. In August 1981, he joined the racing team of Richard Childress. Three years later he would switch from Ford to Chevy. Soon, his black #3 became the most feared car on the track.

Dale wound up with additional Winston Cup titles in 1986, 1987, 1990, 1991, 1993, and 1994. His career total of seven championships tied with Richard Petty's for the most ever.

Dale also finished second in the points race two other times, narrowly missing more glory. He took 76 checkered flags in his career, ranking sixth on NASCAR's all-time list. He also earned better than $40 million, at the time more than any other racer in history.

A smiling Dale Earnhardt? Sure, when he's holding a trophy, as he does here after a 1987 win.

He's also the only stock-car driver to appear on the front of a
Wheaties box. In 1998, he and his father, Ralph, were honored
as two of NASCAR's 50 greatest drivers.

But it wasn't just the number of races or championships
Dale won. It was how long he stayed at the top. Even in 2000,
at the age of 49, he was making people shake their heads.
That year, Dale charged from eighteenth place to win the fall
Winston 500 at Talladega, Alabama. He chased Bobby Labonte
for the Winston Cup title before finishing second.

Dale went to New York to celebrate his 1990 Winston
Cup title. Two mounted park rangers showed up to
inspect his car.

The crazy thing about Dale's career was the trouble he had at the Daytona 500. It surely wasn't the track that gave him headaches. Dale won 29 races in three different divisions at Daytona International Speedway, more than any other driver.

But when it came to the 500, the first (and probably biggest) event of each NASCAR season, fate worked against Dale. In 1986, he was a nose behind leader Geoff Bodine with three laps to go, and he ran

Dale (bottom left) took his racing skills to Indy, when he raced in the 1993 Brickyard 400.

out of gas. In 1990, he was leading when he cut a tire on a piece of metal, less than 1 mile (1.6 kilometers) from the finish line.

Finally, on his twentieth try, Dale won the Daytona 500 in 1998. When the checkered flag waved, more than 100 crew members from other teams jumped the pit wall to congratulate him as he drove to **Victory Lane.** Fans then poured out of the stands to collect pieces of dirt and grass as souvenirs.

The Daytona 500 was stubborn, but not as stubborn as Dale Earnhardt.

In 1998, Dale broke the Daytona jinx. After many near-misses, he finally saw the checkered flag.

THE MAGIC NUMBER

Dale Earnhardt's number 3 Goodwrench Chevy became one of the most famous sights in auto racing. In fact, there's an old joke that says school kids in North Carolina learn to count by repeating, "One, two, Dale Earnhardt, four, five, six. . . ."

CHAPTER THREE

Just a Good Old Boy

If there was anything Dale Earnhardt loved as much as racing or his family, it was the great outdoors. He lived on a 1,000-acre (405-hectare) ranch outside of Mooresville, North Carolina, not far from his childhood home. There he raised cattle and chickens, and kept horses for trail rides.

Dale was crazy about hunting, too. After winning the Winston Cup championship in 1994, he celebrated by flying to New Mexico to join an elk hunt on an Indian reservation. He even had his own special hunting trick.

"A day or two before going hunting, I put the clothes I plan to wear in a plastic trash bag," he told the *Charlotte Observer*. "Then I throw a bunch of pine cones and leaves out of the woods in there and hang the bag outside in the air. My clothing absorbs the smell of the pine cones and leaves."

Dale also enjoyed spending time with his wife, Teresa, and his four children.

But put him in the driver's seat, and this easygoing man suddenly turned to stone.

In 1982, Dale fractured his knee in a crash at Talladega. He didn't miss a single race. He wouldn't let pain stand in his way. And he wasn't always crazy about rules, either. In 1983,

Dale was even more devoted to his wife Teresa and their family than he was to racing.

17

he was fined $10,000 for ignoring a **black flag** in the Clash, a special race at Daytona. A racer shown a black flag must leave the race immediately. (Two days later, officials lowered the fine to $5,000.) When Dale's car builder, Bud Moore, was asked about the incident, he said, "He's a high-strung **thoroughbred.** Dale has this urge to run over everything in his way to get to the front."

Dale couldn't really argue. "I want to give more than a hundred percent every race," he once noted, "and if that's

Dale didn't even let other racers get in the way. Here he bumps Bobby Hamilton out of his path.

aggressive, then I reckon I am."

It is said that the most frightening sight in racing was that Goodwrench number 3, coming fast in your rearview mirror. Dale was fearless in going three (or even four) cars wide on the track, and he never shied away from contact. "There was a time when you'd see a twenty-car pileup," fellow driver Kyle Petty said, "and if just one car made it through, it was the one Earnhardt was driving."

Fans loved Dale's pedal-to-the-metal style. But it didn't

Fans showed their appreciation for Dale's nose-to-nose racing style by making him their favorite.

always win friends among the other drivers.

"When a man pulls over and lets you beside him, then tries to run you into the wall, is that racin'?" Bill Elliott asked after getting bumped at Charlotte in 1987.

That was the year Goodwrench became Dale's sponsor. He was already the Intimidator. Now he became the Man in Black, which was Goodwrench's color, and his legend only grew.

GET YOUR KICKS ON ROUTE 136

In front of Teresa Earnhardt's home along Highway 136 in North Carolina, stands a lasting tribute to Dale's success. It's a huge garage complex and showroom that the racer built. The main building is larger than two football fields. As a comparison, most houses are smaller than the end zone. This "temple" to race cars is so impressive that people call it the **Garage Mahal.**

The Earnhardt Museum near Earnhardt's home boasts equipment such as this racing helmet.

A Dark Day for Racing

T he day of February 18, 2001, will always be a sad occasion to racing fans. Strangely, it very nearly became one of the sport's most joyous dates.

About 175,000 fans crammed into Daytona International Speedway for the 2001 Daytona 500. Millions more watched on TV. The race's Nielsen rating of 10.1 was the highest ever for the event.

From start to finish, Dale Earnhardt was in the middle of the action. The two announcers for the FOX network were Darrell Waltrip and Larry McReynolds. Waltrip had been one of Dale's biggest rivals early in their careers, but they had later grown close. Waltrip called Dale his "frenemy." He said

Dale was 90 percent friend and 10 percent enemy. McReynolds had been Dale's crew chief for two years.

Dale held the lead three times during the race, for a total of 14 laps. He no longer held the front position on the final lap, but he must have been pretty satisfied. He was in third place, and the two racers ahead of him were his employees! Dale still raced for Richard Childress. But he had also started his own team, Dale Earnhardt Incorporated (DEI). Michael Waltrip, Darrell's son, was making his debut in Dale's third car. He was holding the lead. In second place was another

Dale Jr. was smiling before the race, but he cried with everyone else afterward.

Early in the race, Dale (bottom right) found himself
again at the head of the pack.

DEI racer—Dale Earnhardt Jr.

On the final turn of the final lap, Dale slowed down a bit to protect the leaders from anyone trying to pass them. That's when tragedy struck. Sterling Marlin's car touched Dale's. Dale edged left, then shot off to the right. He hit the wall at the same time that his car was struck by Ken Schrader's yellow Pontiac.

Dale's familiar number 3 wound up on the infield grass.

In a split-second, one of racing's greatest careers was over.

Rescue workers rushed him to the hospital, but doctors could not save him. Michael Waltrip's first NASCAR win was over-shadowed by the death of his idol.

The Earnhardt family held a private ceremony to honor Dale. A week later, about 4,500 people gathered for a public

Michael Waltrip's victory in the 2001 Daytona 500 will always be bittersweet.

In the darkness of Dale's last day, fans silently grieved outside their hero's trailer.